POPULATION
Infographics

Chris Oxlade

Chicago, Illinois

To contact Capstone Global Library, please
call 800-747-4992, or visit our web site
www.capstonepub.com

Edited by Rebecca Rissman, Dan Nunn, and John-Paul Wilkins
Designed by Philippa Jenkins
Original illustrations © Capstone Global Library Ltd 2014
Illustrations by HL Studios
Picture research by Elizabeth Alexander
Production by Vicki Fitzgerald
Originated by Capstone Global Library Ltd
Printed and bound in China

17 16 15 14 13
10 9 8 7 6 5 4 3 2 1

Library of Congress Cataloging-in-Publication Data
Oxlade, Chris.
  Population / Chris Oxlade.
     pages cm.—(Infographics)
  Includes bibliographical references and index.
  ISBN 978-1-4109-6218-8 (hardback)—ISBN 978-1-4109-
6223-2 (paperback) 1. Graphic methods—Juvenile literature.
2. Charts, diagrams, etc.—Juvenile literature. 3. Population—
Juvenile literature. 4. Demography—Juvenile literature. I. Title.
  QA90.O958 2014
  304.6072'8—dc23   2013012535

Acknowledgments
We would like to thank the following for permission to
reproduce photographs: Capstone Global Library p. 4;
Shutterstock pp. 4 (© M.Stasy, © Pakhnyushcha, © Stella
Caraman, © Thomas Bethge).

We would like to thank Diana Bentley and Marla Conn for
their invaluable help in the preparation of this book.

Every effort has been made to contact copyright holders
of any material reproduced in this book. Any omissions
will be rectified in subsequent printings if notice is given to
the publisher.

Disclaimer
All the Internet addresses (URLs) given in this book were valid
at the time of going to press. However, due to the dynamic
nature of the Internet, some addresses may have changed, or
sites may have changed or ceased to exist since publication.
While the author and publisher regret any inconvenience this
may cause readers, no responsibility for any such changes
can be accepted by either the author or the publisher.

CONTENTS

Some words are shown in bold, **like this**. You can find out what they mean by looking in the glossary.

ABOUT INFOGRAPHICS

An infographic is a picture that gives you information. Infographics can be graphs, charts, maps, or other sorts of pictures. The infographics in this book are about **population**.

Infographics make information easier to understand. We see infographics all over the place, every day. They appear in books, in newspapers, on television, on web sites, on posters, and in advertisements.

Here's a simple infographic about how many people there are in the world.

World population

7.1 billion
people

7.1 billion
people would fill
860 cities like New York

7.1 billion
people would fill
89,000 Olympic stadiums

WORLD POPULATION

The population of different continents

This map shows how many people live on each of the world's continents. Antarctica is not included because very few people live there!

North America
546 million

South America
396 million

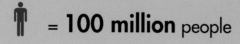 = **100 million** people

Asia is by far
the most heavily
populated continent.

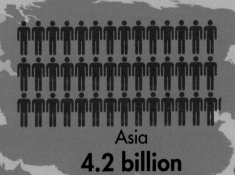

Europe
740 million

Asia
4.2 billion

Africa
1.1 billion

Australia
37 million

The world's growing population

The growing planet Earth in this infographic shows how the world's population has grown in the last 1,000 years.

1.6
1900

1
1800

0.6
1700

0.5
1600

7.1
2013

0.45
1500

The number below each globe shows the year. The number above each globe shows the population in **billions**.

0.4
1400

0.35
1300

0.3
1200

0.25
1100

0.2
1000

The future population

The world's population is growing all the time. This chart shows how the world's population might grow by the year 2100.

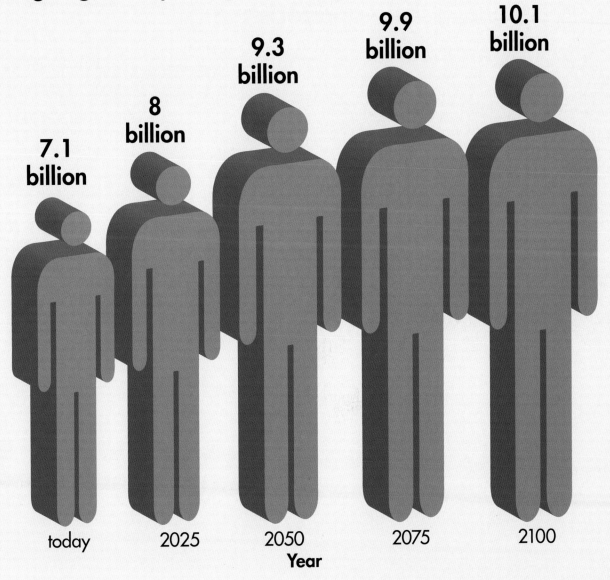

10.1 billion

9.9 billion

9.3 billion

8 billion

7.1 billion

today   2025   2050   2075   2100

Year

COUNTRIES AND CITIES

Countries with the most people

This map shows the 10 countries with the biggest populations in the world today.

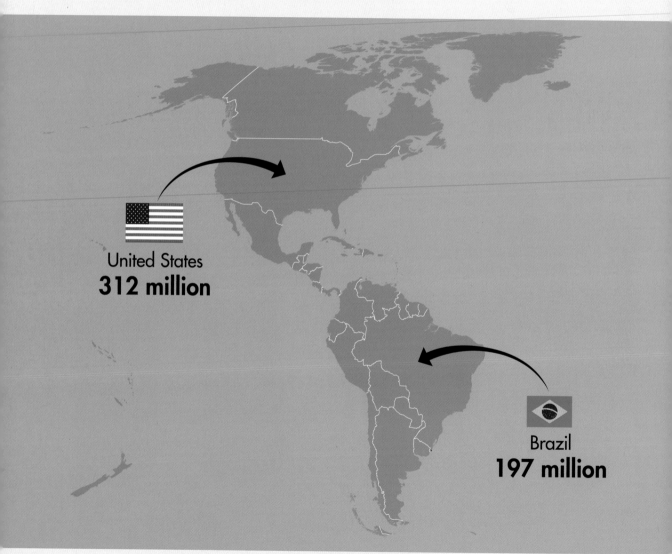

United States
312 million

Brazil
197 million

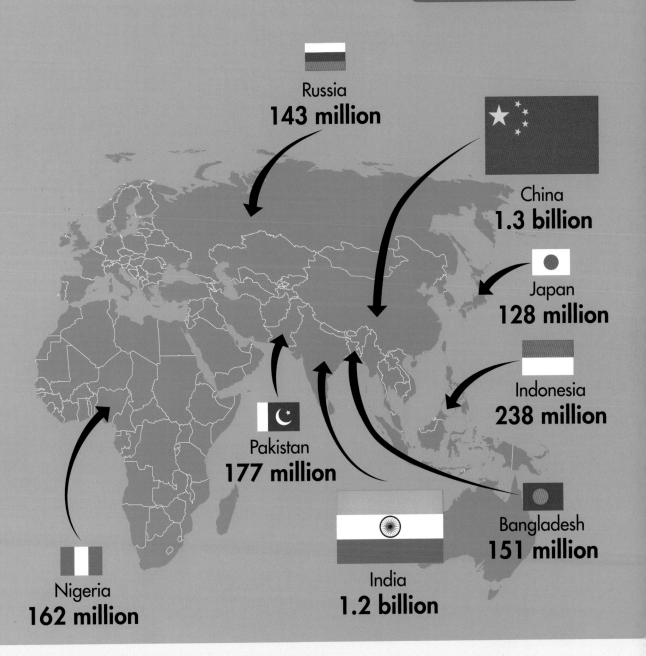

The sizes of the flags show how big the populations are.

Russia
143 million

China
1.3 billion

Japan
128 million

Indonesia
238 million

Pakistan
177 million

Bangladesh
151 million

Nigeria
162 million

India
1.2 billion

Growing countries

In some countries, the population is growing fast. This map shows some of the countries that are growing the fastest.

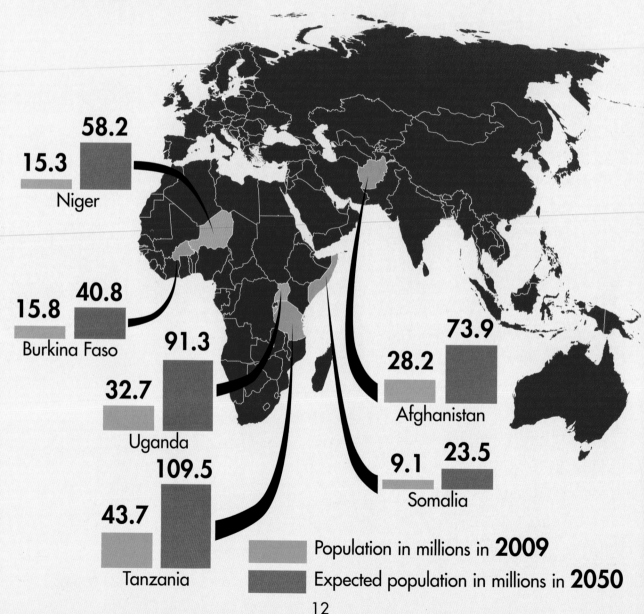

Niger — 15.3 · 58.2

Burkina Faso — 15.8 · 40.8

Uganda — 32.7 · 91.3

Tanzania — 43.7 · 109.5

Afghanistan — 28.2 · 73.9

Somalia — 9.1 · 23.5

Population in millions in **2009**

Expected population in millions in **2050**

Crowded countries and empty countries

Some countries are very crowded. Lots of people are squeezed into a small area. We say they are densely populated. This map shows the most densely populated countries.

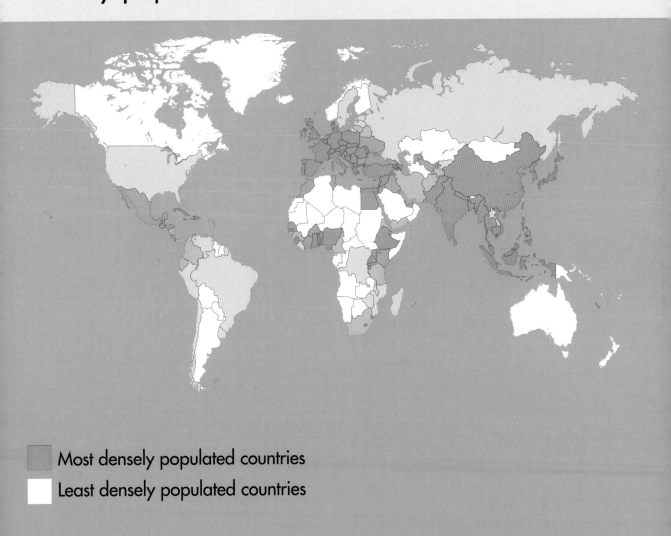

Most densely populated countries

Least densely populated countries

The biggest cities

This map shows the 10 cities in the world that have the biggest populations. The data comes from the **United Nations**.

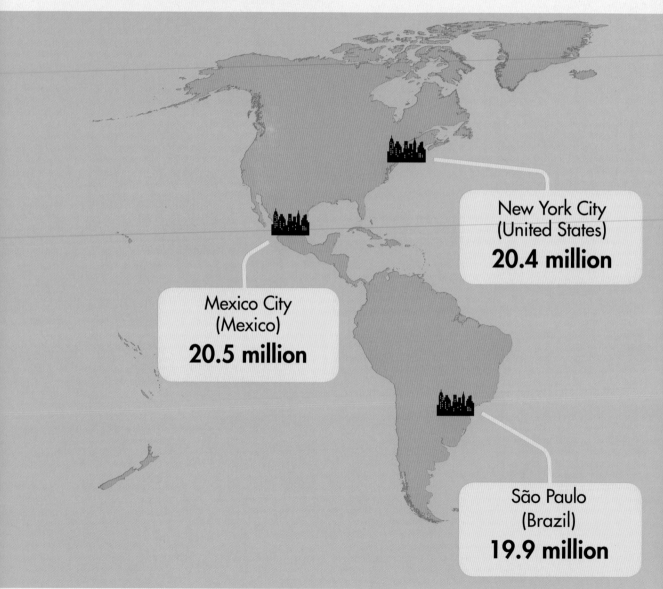

New York City
(United States)
20.4 million

Mexico City
(Mexico)
20.5 million

São Paulo
(Brazil)
19.9 million

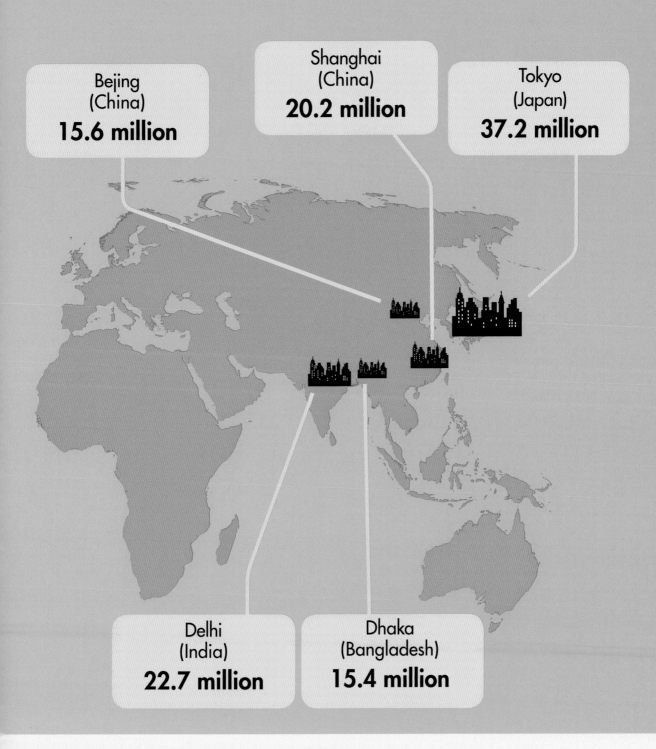

Bejing
(China)
15.6 million

Shanghai
(China)
20.2 million

Tokyo
(Japan)
37.2 million

Delhi
(India)
22.7 million

Dhaka
(Bangladesh)
15.4 million

Cities growing up

This graph shows how the populations of New York City and London grew from 1800 until 2010. These huge cities started out as tiny villages.

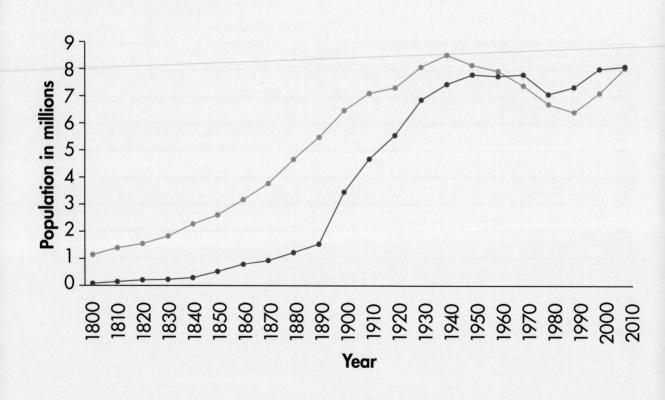

How big in the future?

As the world's populations grow, the world's cities will grow, too. This chart shows how quickly the city of Lagos in Nigeria might grow in the future.

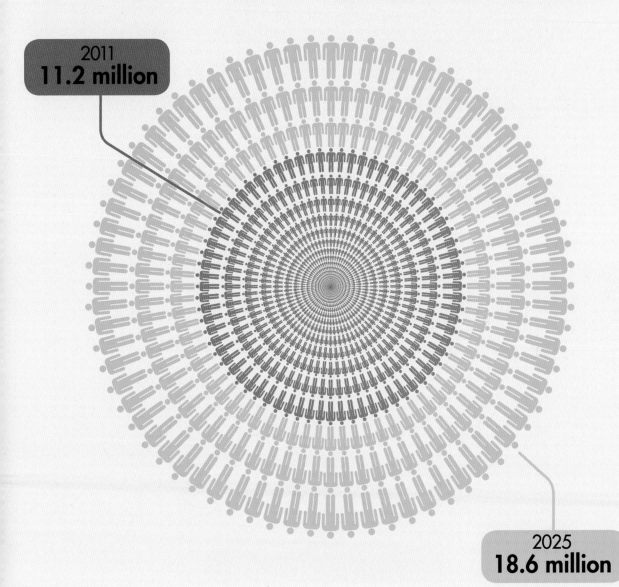

2011
11.2 million

2025
18.6 million

GENDER, AGE, AND LIFE EXPECTANCY

Men and women in the world

This infographic shows that there are almost the same number of males (men and boys) in the world as there are females (women and girls).

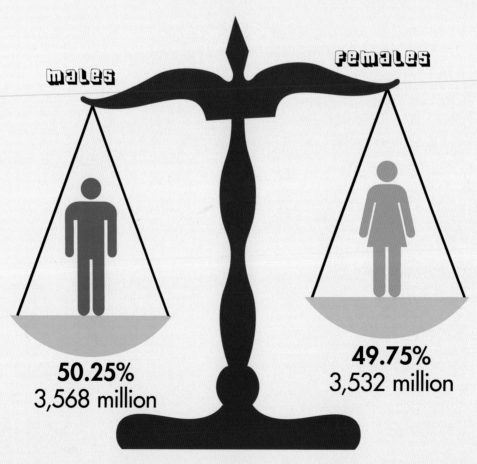

males

females

50.25%
3,568 million

49.75%
3,532 million

How old are people?

This chart shows how many young, middle-aged, and older people there are in the United States.

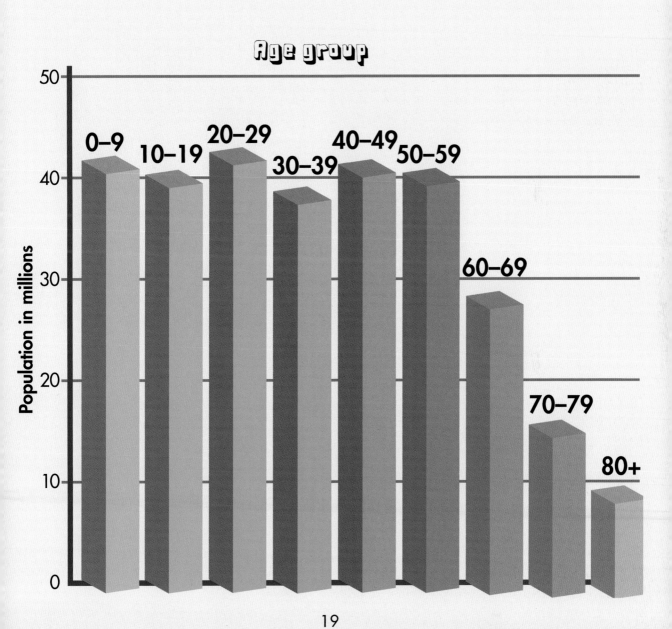

Children and adults

This map shows you how many adults and how many children there are in each continent.

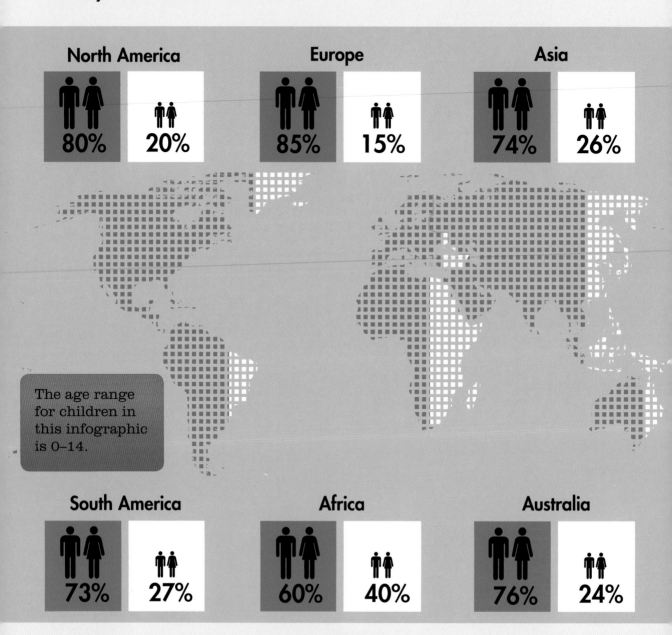

North America

80% 20%

Europe

85% 15%

Asia

74% 26%

The age range for children in this infographic is 0–14.

South America

73% 27%

Africa

60% 40%

Australia

76% 24%

How long people live

This chart shows you how many years people live (called life expectancy) in the United States (U.S.) and the United Kingdom (U.K.).

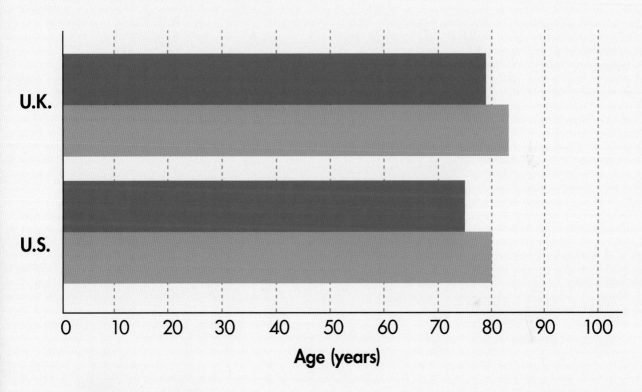

Age (years)

Men   Women

The longest and shortest lives

This map shows the countries where people live the longest lives and the shortest lives.

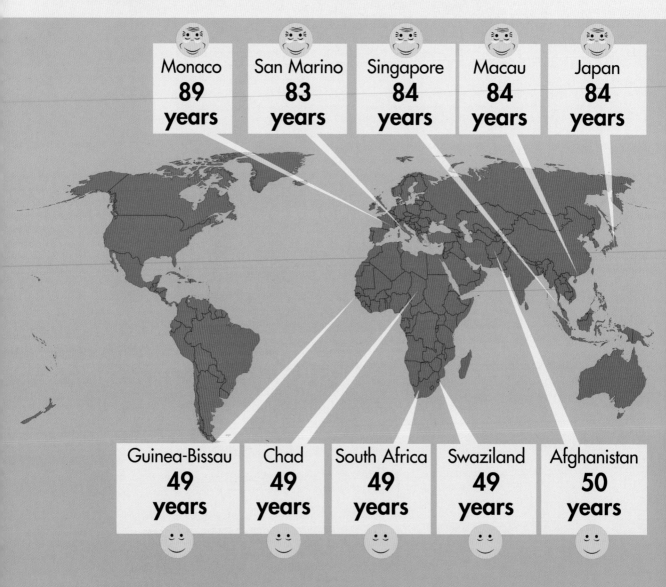

Monaco
89
years

San Marino
83
years

Singapore
84
years

Macau
84
years

Japan
84
years

Guinea-Bissau
49
years

Chad
49
years

South Africa
49
years

Swaziland
49
years

Afghanistan
50
years

Living for longer

How long people normally live is called their life expectancy. This infographic shows how life expectancy has changed in the United States since 1900. Life expectancy is improving because medicine is getting better.

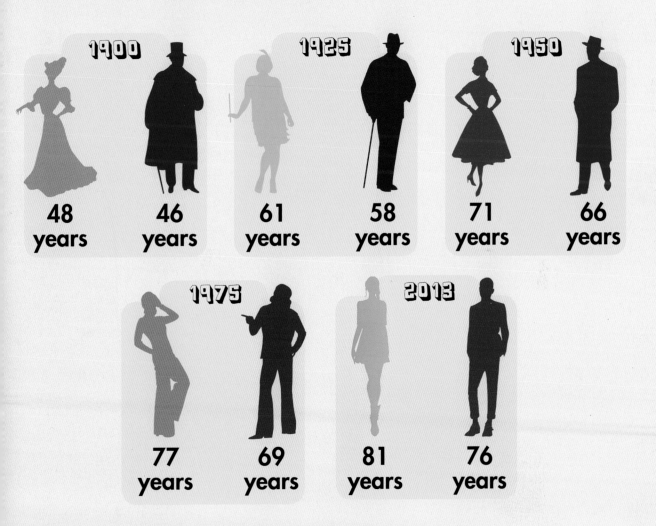

1900
48 years
46 years

1925
61 years
58 years

1950
71 years
66 years

1975
77 years
69 years

2013
81 years
76 years

LANGUAGE AND WRITING

Most common languages

People around the world speak hundreds of different languages. This infographic shows which languages are most commonly spoken.

Mandarin Chinese **12.4%**

Spanish **4.8%**

English **4.8%**

Arabic **3.3%**

Hindi **2.7%**

Bengali **2.7%**

Portuguese **2.6%**

Russian **2.1%**

Japanese **1.8%**

Standard German **1.3%**

Figures are shown as a percentage of the global **population**.

Reading and writing

In some countries, nearly everyone can read and write. In other countries, there are many people who can't read and write. This bar chart shows how many people can read and write in different countries.

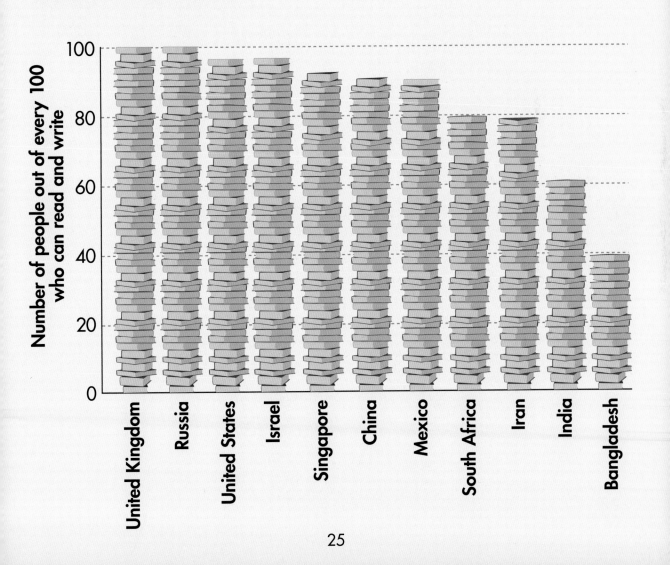

ETHNIC GROUPS

In many countries, the people come from a mixture of **ethnic groups**. These **pie charts** show the ethnic groups of the people who live in the United States, England and Wales, and Australia.

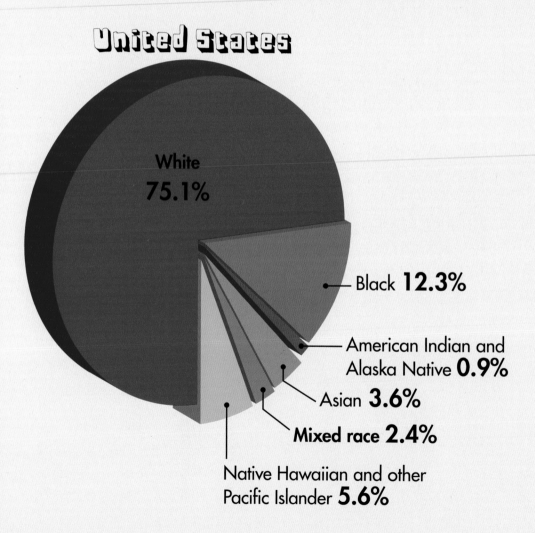

United States

White **75.1%**

Black **12.3%**

American Indian and Alaska Native **0.9%**

Asian **3.6%**

Mixed race **2.4%**

Native Hawaiian and other Pacific Islander **5.6%**

England and Wales

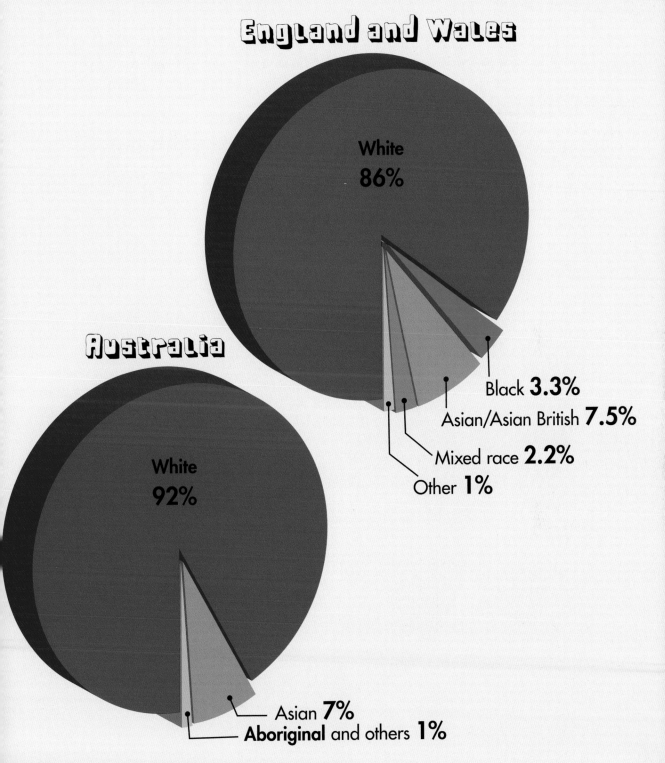

White
86%

Black **3.3%**

Asian/Asian British **7.5%**

Mixed race **2.2%**

Other **1%**

Australia

White
92%

Asian **7%**

Aboriginal and others **1%**

RELIGION AND BELIEF

Most popular religions

There are many different religions in the world. Some are more popular than others. This pie chart shows the most popular religions in the world.

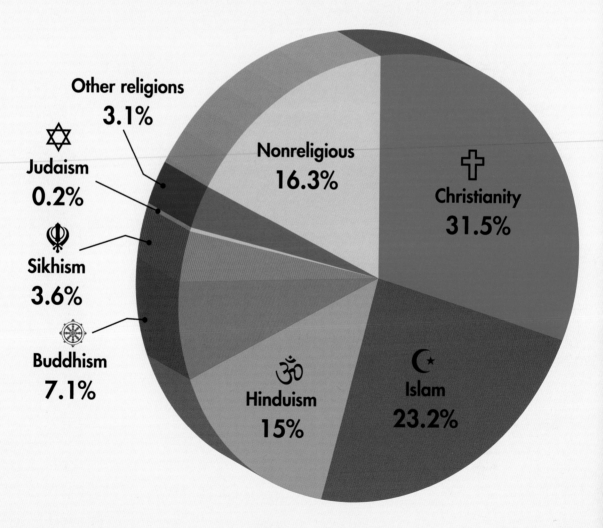

Other religions
3.1%

Judaism
0.2%

Sikhism
3.6%

Buddhism
7.1%

Nonreligious
16.3%

Christianity
31.5%

Hinduism
15%

Islam
23.2%

Popular religions

This bar chart shows the most popular religions in the United States and England and Wales.

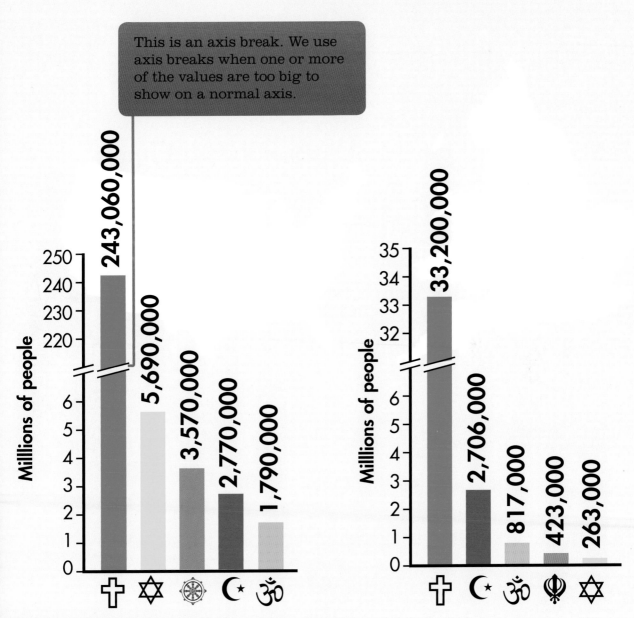

This is an axis break. We use axis breaks when one or more of the values are too big to show on a normal axis.

GLOSSARY

Aboriginal person who belongs to the native people of Australia

billion number that is equal to one thousand times one million; 1,000,000,000

ethnic group group of people of the same race or nationality

mixed race describes someone with ancestors from two or more different ethnic groups

pie chart circular chart that shows how something is divided up by showing pieces of a pie

population people who live in a place; number of people who live in a place

United Nations international organization made up of most of the countries in the world

FIND OUT MORE

Books

Bodach, Vijaya. Making Graphs (series). Mankato, Minn.: Capstone, 2008.

Chambers, Catherine. *Earth's Growing Population* (Headline Issues). Chicago: Heinemann Library, 2008.

National Geographic Kids World Atlas. Washington, D.C.: National Geographic, 2010.

Web sites

Facthound offers a safe, fun way to find web sites related to this book. All the sites on Facthound have been researched by our staff.
Here's all you do:
Visit www.facthound.com
Type in this code: 9781410962188

INDEX